9/09

DEMCO

D1402942

THUMBELINA
The World's Smallest Horse

INSPIRING ANIMALS

HEATHER C. HUDAK

Weigl Publishers Inc.

Published by Weigl Publishers Inc.
350 5th Avenue, Suite 3304, PMB 6G
New York, NY 10118-0069

Website: www.weigl.com

Library of Congress Cataloging-in-Publication Data

Hudak, Heather C., 1975-
Thumbelina : inspiring animals / Heather C. Hudak.
       p. cm.
 Includes index.
 ISBN 978-1-59036-855-8 (soft cover : alk. paper) --
 ISBN 978-1-59036-854-1 (hard cover : alk. paper)
 1. Thumbelina (Horse)--Juvenile literature.
 2. Miniature horses--Missouri--St. Louis--Biography--Juvenile
literature. I. Title.
 SF293.M56H83 2009
 636.1'090929--dc22

                          2008015570

Printed and bound in the United States of America
1 2 3 4 5 6 7 8 9 0   12 11 10 09 08

All of the Internet URLs given in the book were valid at the time
of publication. However, due to the dynamic nature of the
Internet, some addresses may have changed, or sites may have
ceased to exist since publication. While the author and
publisher regret any inconvenience this may cause readers, no
responsibility for any such changes can be accepted by either
the author or the publisher.

PHOTO CREDITS:
Goose Creek Farms: pages 1, 3 bottom, 4, 6, 7, 8 top, 12, 14, 15,
16, 17, 18, 19, 20, 21
Getty Images: pages 3 top, 8 bottom, 9 top left, 9 top right,
9 bottom left, 10, 11, 13

Every reasonable effort has been made to trace ownership
and to obtain permission to reprint copyright material. The
publishers would be pleased to have any errors or omissions
brought to their attention so that they may be corrected in
subsequent printings.

Editor: Leia Tait
Design: Terry Paulhus
Consultant: Michael, Paul, and Kay Goessling

Contents

10

20

Who is Thumbelina?

Thumbelina is a miniature horse, or a mini. Most miniature horses are between 28 and 38 inches (71 and 97 centimeters) tall at the **withers**. Thumbelina is a miniature horse that is also a **dwarf**. She is much smaller than other miniature horses. She is only 17.5 inches (44.5 cm) tall. Thumbelina is the smallest horse in the world.

As a dwarf mini, Thumbelina has faced many challenges. She has had to overcome her tiny size just to survive. With determination and courage, Thumbelina has been able to lead a remarkable life. She has accomplished many things other horses could not.

Thumbelina is named after a character in a fairy tale written by Hans Christian Andersen. Like the character, Thumbelina has had to overcome many obstacles.

Being Brave Thumbelina has faced her challenges bravely. This can be difficult. Think about some challenges that you have faced. How did you show courage in these situations? What did you learn about yourself?

Thumbelina lives on Goose Creek Farms. This is a miniature horse farm near St. Louis, Missouri. The farm is owned by Paul and Kay Goessling. About 50 other miniature horses live on the farm with Thumbelina. Each of the horses is special, but Thumbelina is the Goessling's favorite.

Missouri is located in the central United States. St. Louis is the state's second-largest city. It sits on the bank of the Mississippi River.

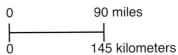

A Difficult Beginning

Thumbelina was born on May 1, 2001. At birth, Thumbelina weighed 8.5 pounds (3.9 kilograms). She was 10 inches (25.4 cm) tall. This is about the size of a full-grown Chihuahua dog. It is very small, even for a miniature horse. Most baby minis, or foals, weigh about 15 to 25 pounds (6.5 to 11.5 kg) at birth. They stand about 16 to 22 inches (40 to 55 cm).

Kay Goessling gave Thumbelina the love and care she needed to survive.

At birth, Thumbelina weighed about the same as a newborn human baby.

The Goesslings were worried. Thumbelina seemed fragile because of her size. Most foals begin to walk and drink their mother's milk within one hour of being born. Thumbelina was so tiny that she had trouble nursing. The Goesslings worried that Thumbelina would not live long.

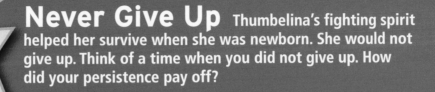

Never Give Up Thumbelina's fighting spirit helped her survive when she was newborn. She would not give up. Think of a time when you did not give up. How did your persistence pay off?

Thumbelina proved everyone wrong. She was determined to survive. With the help of the Goesslings, Thumbelina became healthy and strong. Today, she lives a perfectly normal horse's life on the farm. Away from the farm, however, Thumbelina's life is extraordinary.

Meet the Goesslings

Paul and Kay Goessling are Thumbelina's owners. They care for Thumbelina when she is at Goose Creek Farms. Their son, Michael, is Thumbelina's **handler**. Michael is responsible for Thumbelina's well-being. He looks after Thumbelina when they travel. He is her friend and caregiver.

All about Minis

1 year old

At age one, miniature horses are called yearlings. They are nearly full-grown. When Thumbelina was one year old, she stopped growing. She was the smallest yearling the Goesslings had ever seen. They realized that Thumbelina might be more special because of her size.

Adult

Miniature horses live to be about 25 years of age. As minis age, they become less active. They may develop arthritis. This is a disease that causes the **joints** to stiffen, swell, and ache. Dwarf horses often age faster than other minis, but Thumbelina is strong and healthy.

3 years old

When miniature horses are three years of age, they can have babies of their own. Although Thumbelina is now old enough to have babies, the Goesslings have decided not to **breed** her. Since Thumbelina is so small, having a baby might be dangerous. Thumbelina is very healthy, but dwarfism can sometimes cause problems in minis. Thumbelina could pass down her dwarfism to her babies. The Goesslings want all their horses to be as healthy as can be.

A Closer Look

Eyes

Minis have excellent eyesight. Their eyes are located on the sides of their heads, so they can see nearly all the way around themselves. They can also see well at night.

Hoofs

Miniature horses do not wear horseshoes. Their hoofs are too thin to put nails into, so shoes cannot stay on.

Ears
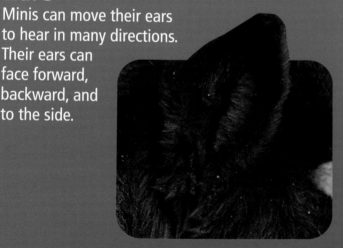
Minis can move their ears to hear in many directions. Their ears can face forward, backward, and to the side.

Teeth

Minis have big teeth, but small mouths. This often causes an **overbite** or an **underbite**. Thumbelina has an underbite.

Becoming a Star

Growing up, Michael Goessling was always interested in Guinness World Records. Since the 1950s, Guinness World Records has been documenting record holders in many different fields. Records include the world's smallest submarine, the longest book title, and the most hot dogs eaten in 10 minutes.

One day, Michael was looking at the Guinness World Records website. According to the site, the world's smallest horse was 3 inches (10 cm) taller than Thumbelina. The Goesslings wrote to Guinness World Records to tell them about Thumbelina.

Michael Goessling helps Thumbelina share her story around the world.

Sizing it Up

Imagine being the same height as Thumbelina. How would your life be different from today? What difficulties would you face? What advantages might you have over others who were taller than you?

In July 2006, the Goesslings received a certificate from Guinness World Records in the mail. Thumbelina was officially the world's smallest horse. Soon, people all over the world began contacting Goose Creek Farms. They wanted to learn more about the amazing Thumbelina.

Radical Records

Look at the animals listed below. In your notebook, list each of them in order from the smallest to the largest. Each of these animals is also a Guinness World Record holder. Do you know which records they hold? Read the answers to find out.

African elephant   bee hummingbird
North African ostrich   cheetah
Madagascar radiated tortoise   blue whale

Answers: 1. The bee hummingbird is the smallest bird. 2. The Madagascar radiated tortoise lives longer than any other animal. 3. The cheetah is the fastest mammal. 4. The North African ostrich is the fastest and biggest land bird. 5. The African elephant is the heaviest land animal. 6. The blue whale is the largest and loudest animal on Earth.

Thumbelina at Home

Like most miniature horses, Thumbelina lives on a farm. During the day, Thumbelina spends a great deal of time exploring outdoors. She is so small that she can crawl under fences and into the **corral**. Thumbelina roams the farm freely and grazes in the backyard.

Miniature horses usually have a barn stall where they eat and sleep. Most stalls are at least 10 feet (3 m) long and 5 feet (1.5 m) wide. Thumbelina has her own large stall, but she prefers to sleep in a doghouse next to the other miniature horse stalls. The doghouse makes her feel safe and cozy.

Thumbelina's doghouse looks like a small igloo.

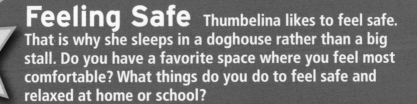

Feeling Safe Thumbelina likes to feel safe. That is why she sleeps in a doghouse rather than a big stall. Do you have a favorite space where you feel most comfortable? What things do you do to feel safe and relaxed at home or school?

Thumbelina eats the same foods as average-sized horses, including hay and oats. However, she eats a smaller amount. A horse weighing 1,000 pounds (454 kg) eats about 20 to 25 pounds (9 to 11 kg) of food each day. A miniature horse eats about 2 to 4 pounds (1 to 2 kg) of food per day. Thumbelina eats much less. She has just 1 cup (250 milliliters) of grain and a handful of hay twice each day. She also grazes on grass around the farm. Sometimes, Thumbelina snacks on apples and carrots.

Like other horses, Thumbelina eats a mix of grains. For a treat, she eats fruits and vegetables.

Staying Healthy

In winter, Thumbelina's hair grows long to keep her warm.

Grooming is an important part of Thumbelina's health. To keep Thumbelina's coat clean, the Goesslings brush her often. They also bathe her with a garden hose. Thumbelina does not enjoy having a bath. It is one of her least favorite activities.

In winter, Thumbelina's dark brown coat grows thick to keep her warm. In summer, her coat will shed. Since the weather in Missouri can be quite warm, Thumbelina's coat is shaved to keep her cool. When her hair is short, it is possible to see light brown polka dots on Thumbelina's back and stomach.

Different is Good Compare Thumbelina to other miniature horses. In your notebook, list some of the differences that make her special. Think about the people in your life. Do you know someone with a story like Thumbelina's? What has he or she done to overcome obstacles?

Overcoming Obstacles

Like many dwarf minis, Thumbelina was born with crooked legs. This can make walking difficult and painful. To help, Thumbelina wears special shoes that give her support where she needs it. They keep her back and neck in line.

Thumbelina's special shoes are nothing like typical horseshoes, which are made of metal. Her shoes are made from a special **acrylic** mixture. Every six weeks, a **farrier** fits Thumbelina with new shoes. She lies on a table while the farrier coats her hoofs with liquid. As it hardens, the mixture molds to Thumbelina's hoofs. When her shoes are dry, Thumbelina can walk and play more comfortably. The farrier is gentle, and the shoes do not hurt Thumbelina.

Thumbelina relaxes while the farrier makes her shoes.

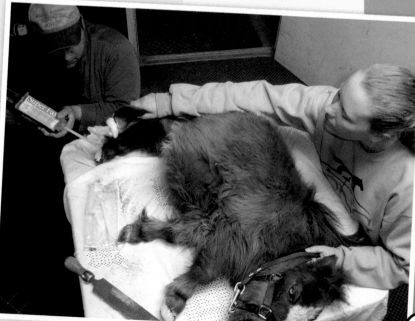

15

Thrilling Thumbelina

Thumbelina is the alpha horse at Goose Creek Farms. This means that she is in charge of the other horses. Even though she is small, Thumbelina is not afraid to be a leader. She will boss around the biggest horses. Thumbelina is confident in herself, so the other horses respect her. They follow her. Thumbelina never lets her size stop her from taking charge.

Thumbelina loves to play with other horses on the farm. She especially likes playing with the foals that are born each spring, since they are closer to her size.

Thumbelina is not afraid to stand up to much larger horses.

Thumbelina is the only horse on Goose Creek Farms that has never been for sale.

Being in Charge Thumbelina is a natural leader. Think about a time when you had to be in charge. What about it was difficult? What was easy? Do you consider yourself a natural leader? Why or why not?

Thumbelina also enjoys spending time with the dogs at Goose Creek Farms. Together, they explore the farm, play in the fields, and lounge around. As a special treat, Thumbelina goes for car rides. She loves to look out the window as she sits in the back.

A Special Friend

Thumbelina has many dog friends, but one is very special. Castica, or Cassie, is an Estrella Mountain dog. She lives at Goose Creek Farms and acts as Thumbelina's guardian. Cassie is twice Thumbelina's size. When Cassie senses danger, such as coyotes, she barks to scare away potential **predators** and warn the Goesslings and the horses. Cassie and Thumbelina are best friends. They even share each other's food.

17

Giving Back

Thumbelina's small size is only one of the things that make her special. She is also a great friend to children everywhere. Thumbelina travels great distances each year to bring joy to countless children throughout North America. Thumbelina visits children's hospitals, schools, camps, fairs, zoos, horse shows, and other places. She enjoys spending time with people and loves when they pet her.

Thumbelina has a way of bringing happiness and comfort to those who need it most. She often approaches people with illnesses and disabilities. Thumbelina will stay near these individuals throughout a visit. She will untie their shoelaces and chew on their shirt cuffs to make them feel special.

Thumbelina enjoys meeting children from across the country.

In 2007, the Goesslings created the Thumbelina Charitable Foundation. The foundation helps raise money for children's charities across North America. It also raises awareness about the work these charities perform. Thumbelina helps raise money by encouraging donations and participating in fundraising activities, such as **auctions** and raffles. Money she earns from private appearances goes to the foundation. The foundation's mission is to raise millions of dollars.

The Thumby Mobile

Thumbelina travels in a special **recreational vehicle**, or an RV. Most RVs have a bedroom, bathroom, kitchen, dining area, and living room. In Thumbelina's RV, the back bedroom has been removed, and a stable has been built in its place. The stable is Thumbelina's home away from home. It contains food, bedding, and grooming supplies. Even Thumbelina's doghouse fits inside, so she can travel in comfort. The Goesslings have nicknamed the RV the "Thumby Mobile."

Achievements and Successes

Thumbelina is known around the world. She has been featured in newspapers, such as the *New York Post*, and magazines, such as *Hello* and *In Touch*. She has appeared on television shows around the world, including *Today*, *Good Morning America*, *Live with Regis and Kelly*, *Inside Edition*, *Discovery Channel*, and *The Oprah Winfrey Show*.

Thumbelina has been to many parts of the United States, including Niagara Falls.

In 2007, Thumbelina traveled nearly 40,000 miles to each of the 48 continental states as part of the Thumbelina Children's Tour. The goal of the tour was to visit with sick, needy, troubled, disabled, and abused children throughout North America and raise money for charity. By the end of the tour, Thumbelina had visited more than 20,000 children. She also helped raise tens of thousands of dollars for many charities across North America.

Helping Others Donating to a charity or volunteering for a charitable cause is a good way to help others. Research some charities and volunteer organizations near you. Is there something you can do to help?

During the tour, Thumbelina was awarded for her efforts to help others. She received the "Lifting Up the World With a Oneness-Heart" award from peace **advocate** Sri Chinmoy. The award recognized Thumbelina's work to help children. Sri used a special machine to lift Thumbelina and her handler, Michael, with one hand!

Thumbelina is an inspiration to many people. She has not allowed her small size to hold her back. She has shown that, with hard work and a strong will, it is possible to beat the odds. Thumbelina is proof that everyone can achieve great things.

It was a special day for Thumbelina when she won the "Lifting Up the World With a Oneness-Heart" award in 2007.

Make a Miniature Horse

Materials You Need:
the tube from a toilet paper roll
crayons or colored pencils
scissors
glue
colored paper

Instructions

Cut a piece of colored paper to fit around the tube. Wrap the paper around the tube, and glue it in place.

Draw the shape of a horse's head facing forward on another piece of paper. Draw eyes, a nose, and a mouth on the face.

Cut out the horse's head, and glue it to the front of the tube. The head, eyes, and ears should be above the top of the tube. Draw two front legs on a piece of paper. Be sure to add hoofs.

Cut out the legs, and glue them just below the horse's head.

Draw a long, full tail on a piece of paper.

Cut out the tail, and fold back about 0.25 inches (0.64 cm) on the top to create a tab. Glue the tab to the back of the horse.

Draw two feet on a piece of paper. Cut out the feet, and fold back about 0.25 inches (0.64 cm) to create a tab.

Use a pencil or crayon to draw a 1-inch (2.5-cm) line up from the center of the bottom of the horse to make two legs. Then, glue the tab on the feet to the two legs.

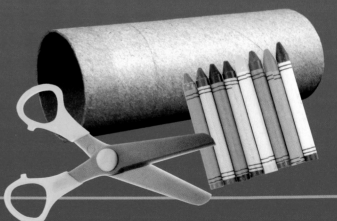

Further Research

Many books and websites provide information about miniature horses. To learn more about miniature horses, borrow books from the library, or surf the Internet.

Books to Read

Most libraries have computers that connect to a database for researching information. If you input a key word, you will be provided with a list of books in the library that contain information on that topic. Non-fiction books are arranged numerically, using their call number. Fiction books are organized alphabetically by the author's last name.

Online Sites

For up-to-date information about Thumbelina, visit www.worldssmallesthorse.com.

To learn more about miniature horses, check out www.amha.org.

Find out about other world record holders at www.guinnessworldrecords.com.

Glossary

acrylic: a type of plastic used to make casts, molded parts, and coatings

advocate: someone who supports a cause

auctions: sales where items are sold to those who offer to pay the most

breed: to mate in order to have babies

corral: a pen for horses, sheep, or cows

dwarf: a person, animal, or plant that is much smaller than average

farrier: a blacksmith who specializes in horseshoes

grooming: keeping clean through bathing, brushing, and related activities

handler: a person who trains and cares for an animal

joints: places where parts of the body connect and bend

overbite: when the top teeth overlap the bottom teeth

predators: animals that hunt other animals for food

recreational vehicle: a type of van that people can camp inside while they travel

underbite: when the bottom teeth overlap the top teeth

withers: the last hairs of a horse's mane near the shoulders

Index